Books by Carol Lynn Pearson

A Christmas Thief

A Sister

A Stranger for Christmas

Beginnings and Beyond

Consider the Butterfly

Day-Old Child

Fuzzy Red Bathrobe

Girlfriend, You Are the Best!

Goodbye, I Love You

I'll Always Be Your Daughter

I'm Still a Hot Babe, But Now It Comes in Flashes

In Love Again and Always

Morning Glory Mother

No More Goodbyes

One on the Seesaw

Picture Window

Summer of Truth

The Christmas Moment

The Christmas Play

The Dance

The Gift

The Lesson

The Model Mormon Mother's Notebook

The Modern Magi

The Runaway Mother

The Sweet, Still Waters of Home

Today, Tomorrow, and Four Weeks from Tuesday

What Love Is

Will You Still Be My Daughter?

The Christmas Moment

The *modern* re-telling *of*
O. Henry's Christmas classic
The Gift of the Magi

ISBN 13: 978-1-4621-1208-1

Published by Sweetwater Books, an imprint of Cedar Fort, Inc.
2373 W. 700 S., Springville, UT, 84663
Distributed by Cedar Fort, Inc., www.cedarfort.com

Cover design by Erica Dixon and Rebecca J. Greenwood

Printed in the United States of America

10 9 8 7 6 5 4 3 2 1

Printed on acid-free paper

The Christmas Moment

The *modern* re-telling *of*
O. Henry's Christmas classic
The Gift of the Magi

CAROL LYNN PEARSON

Sweetwater Books
An imprint of Cedar Fort, Inc.
Springville, Utah

Chapter One

You have learned by this time, I am certain, that the coming of Christmas does not necessarily mean the coming of the spirit of Christmas. Across the land there are hundreds of thousands of spiritless people who need a bit of a miracle in order to receive that blessed gift.

But we cannot tell the story of hundreds of thousands, can we? In story, the general must become particular, as happened that holy night in Bethlehem when God became man. And so we are going to tell the story of one family—four individuals, separated by skin, as we all are, into particular souls. Don't let that separation fool you as it has fooled them. They—and you,

and I, and the godchild we celebrate—are one in that astonishing way that the lights on the tree burst into brilliance through one source.

The Young home displayed a wreath on the front door that was purchased from the Girl Scouts. There was no snow. Blinking white, red, and green bulbs decorated the bushes and the front porch. Inside, on a lace cloth on a card table, was a beautifully carved nativity set purchased in Oberamergau by Grandpa. A Douglas fir tree was strung with tinsel and bright balls. Here and there was holiday handiwork that had the sweet mark of elementary school creativity.

The four souls in our story were very much absorbed in their own particular points of view. Two were in the family room watching *A Charlie Brown Christmas.* Todd, the older of the two at twelve, pretended to be too old for Charlie Brown, but there he was in his stocking feet, sprawled over most of the couch. Liza, the younger at eight, was curled up in her pajamas on the other side of the couch.

"Don't touch me!" That was Liza.

"Then move over!" That was Todd.

"I'm practically falling off the couch now. *You* move over!"

"I was here first."

"Well, I was here *this morning!*"

"Well, I was here *yesterday!*"

This exchange continued until Todd brought up the time that he was brought home from the hospital and his mother sat with him in her arms right there on that couch when Liza wasn't even born yet. Liza grumbled and scowled and scrunched herself farther away from the offending stockinged foot. Clearly, the only one with Christmas spirit in the family room was Charlie Brown.

The other two souls in the Young household were in the front room. Della was sitting at the computer, her fingers idle, staring out the window at a palm tree. James was in the big, black leather chair reading the newspaper.

"What do you want me to say about you?"

That was Della.

"Huh?" That was James.

"What shall I put in the Christmas letter?"

"You're doing that again, huh?"

"Yes, I'm doing that again. I seem to be the only one who cares. What do you want me to say?"

"I don't care."

"Care about what?"

"What you say. Tell them I lost my job."

"Can't you think of anything cheerful? We really need to put something cheerful in the Christmas letter, don't you think?"

"I didn't get run over by a truck." James turned the page of the newspaper and did not look up.

Della sighed and turned back to the computer screen.

That is what things looked like that night in the Young household. The amount of Christmas spirit could have been put inside a ball on the tree, and it still would have rattled. But don't be deceived by what things look like. We have

peeked inside the rooms to take a look at the people. Let us now peek inside the people—the real world beyond the world of appearances.

When I introduced you to James, who grunted behind the newspaper, you probably saw an overweight, balding, disappointed, and somewhat cynical forty-year-old man. Look closer. Let the magic of Christmas dissolve appearances like warm air dissolves frost on a windowpane. There, do you see? Sitting in that old, leather recliner, is a shining, blindingly magnificent manifestation of the divine, pulsing with light, which is love.

And what about that woman who sits at the computer? I'll bet you're seeing a pretty but slumping woman who needs her hair trimmed and has creases of worry between her listless green eyes. But beneath that, can you see? View the awesome, luminous splendor of her—a holy hologram of the whole and holy universe, a creative thought of God, the purest point of absolute perfection, who is sighing and playing the martyr at her computer.

Likewise, let us turn to the other two muted points of light that make up this family. Yes, that stunning glory sitting in stockinged feet on the couch in the form of an obnoxious twelve year-old boy. View also that breathtaking beauty whining from the pouted lips of an eight-year-old girl.

Now, the thing that should make us laugh, even hoot in disbelief, is that these four points of magnificent light are such competent pretenders that they have fooled not only you, but they have even fooled themselves. They look at each other across the room, they look at themselves in the mirror, and they do not see what they truly are. They only see a dull, temporary surface. And they think they are separate and competitive, and they grunt at each other, saying things like, “Don’t touch me,” or, “Huh? I don’t care.”

We are grateful that this is the beginning of the story and not the end. You are guessing, I expect, that this story, like the larger story that God writes across the glowing skies, will

have a happy ending, and our masqueraders will learn something wonderful. They will come to *see*, and their separation will melt like snow in springtime, changing not only themselves but perhaps the whole world. For, as chaos theory postulates, the flutter of a butterfly's wings in Japan affects the weather on the California coast. Ah, the changing of four human lives is a thunderingly momentous event.

The story could be told through the eyes of either James or Della, but we will see it through the eyes of Della, the wife and mother, because at present she notices the most, seems to care the most, and certainly talks the most.

Chapter Two

The remarkable letter that began the magic did not come the following day. What did come was a handful of Christmas cards, several bills, and four requests from charities. Todd brought them into the kitchen, with Liza running in pursuit. "It was my turn to get the mail! Give it to me!"

"You can't even read it, Dummy!"

"Can too! Mo-om!"

"*Stop it*!" Della said, throwing the dish towel onto the counter and staring scorchingly at her children. "Go to your rooms! Now!"

Muttering, the children skulked away and Della sighed her habitual sigh and sank onto the nearest kitchen chair, picked up the mail, and scanned the return addresses.

A bright red envelope bore the address label of her old college roommate Joan. She always loved to hear from Joan. Della opened the card and took out the folded, duplicate letter and the picture of the family in a smiling hug. She skimmed the family news—job promotion, trip to Hawaii to celebrate their wedding anniversary, youngest child got straight A's in accelerated classes, middle child made Eagle Scout, and oldest child won a scholarship to Harvard and national science prize. "And at this season, what we are most grateful for is each other, to be a family, to know as we sing together around the piano that our hearts are one and now made even more joyful by the birth of the Lord. May the same love abide with you and yours. . . ."

Della sighed again, feeling like the last person picked for sides in volleyball—a loser. Where did she go wrong? Yes, her family loved each other. She knew they would cry at each other's funerals, but where was the joy?

Long after the two children had gone to bed,

Todd smirking and Liza crying because her brother had chased her down the hall with his collection of rubber spiders and snakes, Della sat at the computer. And she sat there long after James had put down the newspaper and stretched and said, "Well, I think I'll go out to the shop for a couple of hours."

"I wish you'd stay here and help me write the Christmas letter," Della had replied.

"Nah. You're better at that than I am. Whatever you write will be fine."

So James went out to the shop. Actually, it was the garage. It was only James who called it the shop; Della made a point of calling it the garage. And she hated the garage. It was worse than another woman. There was no way she could compete with his table saw, plywood, glue gun, and sander.

She told herself he was withdrawing to his "cave," like she had read about in that book—a place where men need to go to be alone, to be men, to do their manly thing or nurse their

wounds, to be quiet and not have to talk. He seemed to be withdrawing to his cave more and more, especially this last year after he lost his job with a computer firm because of cutbacks and was temporarily working for the insurance company of a friend at church.

Even when he was not in his cave he seemed to be thinking about it. Occasionally he would look up from the newspaper he was reading and his eyes would light up for the first time in quite a while and he would say, "When I get some money, that's what I'll get—a table router and a set of high-speed router bits. Add that to my table saw, and I can make real furniture!"

A router. Della hated the word. She'd like to rout James out of the garage, that's what she'd like to do. As she heard the door to the garage close, Della turned back to her computer. *This is how it always is,* she thought. James didn't want to help her with a project like the Christmas letter. He didn't even want to talk to her. It didn't help to remember what she had read in

that other book. The book said that women have hundreds more words in their brains per day than men do, so naturally men run out of words long before women do. Women have all these words left over that they toss out, feeling like they're playing table tennis all by themselves. It still hurt. She had to talk to herself—to look at her own words up there on the lighted, buzzing screen and make conversation with her cursor.

Maybe last year's letter would give her a few ideas. Della opened her filing cabinet and withdrew a fat manila file. *Let's see. Last year's letter, the year before, the year before that. . . .* Suddenly the tears came. The little packet of letters they had written that first Christmas, when they were apart because Della went to Montana to take care of her mother after major surgery. They were love letters. Oh, to feel that way again! She chose one at random and opened it.

"Dearest James, I found the most wonderful present for you while window shopping today, but, alas, you will never see it. Oh, I would sell

my hair to get it! But no one buys short, permed, blond snippets. . . .”

For several years it had been such a fun joke. “Oh, James, James, I would sell my hair for you!”

Della slammed the filing cabinet and brought herself back to dull, loveless reality. What could she write in this year’s Christmas letter? And then she thought, *Does anybody really write the truth?* Their friends Howard and Melanie had divorced this year, and their Christmas letter last year had not given a clue. Della smiled wryly. What if people really wrote the truth?

“Dear Friends.” Her fingers quickly typed the words onto the blank screen. “Greetings from a very sad and confused household. Boy, has this been a rotten year. James and I are not talking divorce yet, but I don’t think he loves me anymore, because he spends all his time in the garage playing with his stupid table saw. Frankly, I feel like I’ve put my feelings for him in storage, farther away than the boxes of Christmas stuff, and now I can’t remember

where they are. I can't remember the last time we laughed together or said anything really sweet to one another. Yes, we pass like ships in the night.

"And the kids—Liza is doing pretty well in remedial reading, and Todd did a good job of repainting the neighbor's fence where he had written some bad words. If I'd known how much quarreling comes with the territory, I don't think I'd have become a mother. Of course, I love them, but sometimes I don't much like them, and I know they'd be better children if they had a better mother.

"Financially things are nearly rock bottom. James lost his job. I finally tried to make a go of the dance studio I'd been dreaming about for years, but it didn't work. At the grocery store I buy a lot of lentils and split peas and no cookies, and it's going to be a real stretch just to get stamps for these letters.

"But the biggest loss of the year . . ."

Della stopped typing as she heard a voice

from down the hall. "Mommy? Mommy!"

"Coming!" Della quickly erased the screen in case James should come in from his cave, and she hurried down the hall.

"What is it, Sweetie?"

"Grandpa won't be here for Christmas, will he?"

Della knelt by the little girl's bed and put a hand on her cheek. "No, Liza. He won't."

That was what Della was about to mention in her "letter." The biggest loss of the year—their Grandpa's death.

"Tell me again why it was okay. Tell me about how he went to heaven."

"Oh, he did, Liza. And who did he see very first off?"

"Grandma."

"And what did she look like?"

"Like a shining angel. And she came running to hug him, and he smiled and smiled, didn't he?"

"He sure did. And what did he say to Grandma?"

"He said, 'Now we'll never, never be apart

again, and I love you as much as all of heaven.'"

"And they're probably dancing together right this minute. Ta-da-da-da—ta-da—ta-da . . ." Della sang the melody she remembered Grandpa always singing as he picked up her babies and danced around the room.

Liza sighed. "But I still wish he was here and not there. It's not going to feel like Christmas without him."

"I know, Sweetie. I know." Della kissed her little girl and left the room. Yes, Liza was a sweetheart. If only she had a better mother.

As Della sat down again at the computer, James was just coming in from his cave. "Guess it's bedtime. You coming?"

"No. I need to spend a few minutes out."

"It's late," James said invitingly.

"I won't be long."

"Oh." He raised a hand and opened his mouth before hesitating and turning away. "Well, then, I guess I'll do a little more work in the shop."

As Della walked outside to her garden, she

pulled the afghan around her. It was chilly but not cold like the Montana winters she had grown up in. Here in Southern California she could have her garden all year round.

James had his shop and Della had her garden. This was her healing place—her sanctuary. It was small but sacred. Nobody else in the family ever came out except to call her to the phone or ask her when supper would be ready. She missed the snow of her childhood, but the compensation for living where it never got really cold was that even in the winter she could have her garden. There were flowering shrubs and carefully placed rocks and her angel. Her angel was marble—*real* marble from Florence, Italy—a lovely, wistfully smiling, two-foot-high angel. Two clear marbles had been placed in the eye sockets, and sometimes, when Della knelt to look her in the face and then rose, she was certain that those eyes followed her. The angel was positioned by the bench that James had built for her when they first married and she knew that he loved her. He had built and polished

the bench as a surprise and had led her out to it blindfolded. When she had gasped in delight, he had swung her down onto his lap and kissed her and said they would come out here all the time and make out under the stars. It had been a long time now since they had made out under the stars. *What a dirty trick falling in love is,* she thought. *It begins in the moonlight and ends in the garage.* Della leaned back and closed her eyes. How would she and James greet one another in heaven?

"Hi, James."

"Oh. Hello. You're here, huh?"

"Yes. May I come in?"

"I don't care."

No. That was rude. Of course he would care. But if you didn't learn joy on earth, could you have it in heaven? She should have asked Grandpa how it was done.

Della had bought the angel downtown at Greeley's Art and Monument when she first made the garden and had a little money of her own, but she didn't have enough to buy the shining marble

stand that went with it. So the angel rested on a little circle of rocks, and sometimes storms left mud on the divine hem of her dress. Every year Della had said to herself that this was the year that she would be able to buy the marble stand that would give her celestial friend a worthy base and make her garden the modestly spectacular place she dreamed of. Beauty! She needed a spot of beauty. James didn't understand that, but she felt she would die without a little spot of beauty in her life.

She occasionally dropped in to Greeley's just to admire the array of angels and cherubs and to examine the stands. Whenever she came in, Mr. Greeley would say, "Is the angel being a good angel?"

"Oh, yes," she would say. "She's being a wonderful angel."

"You're pretty lucky you got that when you did, you know. They're getting harder and harder to come by. I could sell that angel a dozen times over."

There were always beautiful marble stands

there, but certainly this was not the year for it. She knew she would be lucky to make it through Christmas with a few things in the stockings. Her slim paycheck from her job at the rest home that used to go for extras now went for necessities. Months ago, she had managed to put away a training bike for Liza and a set of rollerblades for Todd, and now she only had enough for groceries until the end of the month and just enough to buy James a new sweater.

But that was not what she had come out to her garden to think about. She had come to think about Grandpa, the loss of the year. James's job loss didn't even come close, and neither did the failure of her little dance studio. Early on, when James used to tease, he teased her about marrying him just so she could have his father and mother too. They were the perfect couple. When Della had first met them that time she went home with James for Thanksgiving, she could hardly take her eyes off them. There was a man who looked at his wife with worship in his

soft, blue eyes, and who held her hand as they sat on the couch together. There was a woman who touched her husband fondly whenever she passed him, sometimes even leaning over and kissing the top of his head. When a certain song came on the radio and James's father grabbed his wife in the kitchen and danced her around the front room, amid laughter and protests and the waving of a wooden spoon, Della was amazed. She had never seen people who had been married for a long time act that way, as if they really *loved* each other and couldn't help showing it. James's mother had been dead for a number of years now, and they missed her terribly. Della's own parents had divorced when she was small, and no one had known where her father was for years. Her mother still lived in Montana but refused to fly, so they didn't see her much.

Christmas became Grandpa and Grandma's. James had been an only child, so his parents didn't have to spread themselves around. For

two weeks every December, and often in the summers, two beautiful, delightful, laughing, loving people would arrive and turn the house upside down with fun. How they did it was still a mystery to Della, even though she watched as closely as she watched the magicians on television and even made notes. Christmastime was Grandpa and Grandma time, and the children counted the days. Then it was just Grandpa time, and amazingly, he could spread the joy all by himself with his booming, laughing voice; his tender hugs, jokes, and songs; and his little sacks of chocolate peanut clusters.

But not this year. Grandpa couldn't come because Grandpa was in heaven.

He was spending last February in Egypt and Israel with some other archaeologists from his university, and he suffered a heart attack in Jerusalem. When the phone rang in the middle of the night and they received word, it was as if a light went out that never came back on. That great, wonderful warmth

they knew as Grandpa would never be with them again.

That was the loss of the year. In fact, it was the loss of many years. Della put out a hand and touched the marble angel, which was beautiful but cold. Grandpa was in heaven. James was in his cave. The children were in bed. She was in her garden. And the angel was the only one smiling.

Chapter Three

The next day was the day that the remarkable letter came.

Della had spent the morning in the kitchen, working hard on enjoying making Christmas cookies with the kids. She had put *The Nutcracker* on in the background to try to bring good cheer, but other sounds seemed to drown out the dance of the Sugar Plum Fairy:

"Would you move your dumb doll? She's getting in the way."

"She's helping with the cookies and she is not dumb. You're dumb!"

"All your dolls are dumb. Dumb, dumb dolls!"

"They're smarter than your stupid spiders!"

"Could you two please stop squabbling

for once, and let's have a happy time making cookies?"

"Mom! Todd is eating the dough again!"

"I'm just eating the crumbs."

"There aren't any crumbs, Dummy! They're not even baked yet!"

"*You're* a crumb!"

"Well, you're a *bigger* crumb!"

"Stop it! Stop it right now!" Della wadded up the cookie dough she was rolling out and threw it back onto the moist pile. "I am astonished! I try to do something nice for you two, and what do I get? Fighting, fighting, fighting! Nothing but fighting!"

"He started it!"

"She started it!"

Della picked up the big wooden rolling pin and smashed it down onto the table.

The children jumped. Their mother usually did not smash things or throw things or even get as red in the face as she was right now.

Just then James came in from the garage.

"What's going on in here?" he said with only mild interest. Then, not waiting for an answer, he asked, "Has anybody seen my turpentine? I had some turpentine and now I can't find it."

"James?"

"Yeah?"

Della tried to keep her voice bright and even. "Would you like to help us? With the cookies?"

"It's fun, Daddy!" said Liza.

"He doesn't want to make cookies!" The snort and the statement were from Todd.

"Sure. Sure I do. Just let me finish what I'm doing."

He disappeared out the garage door, and Della knew it would be hours before he finished, and by then the cookies would be done.

Just then they heard the familiar squeak of the mailbox. "I'll get it!" Todd quickly wiped his hands on a dish towel and ran for the front door.

"It's my turn!" Liza was only inches behind him.

Della sat down and sighed. She rolled a few

crumbs of cookie dough into a little ball and put it in her mouth. Maybe after the holidays she would sign up for that stress-reduction class.

After a moment, the children came back into the kitchen—Todd holding a small stack of mail he had been shuffling through and Liza pouting behind him. Then Todd stopped walking and stopped shuffling the mail and just stared.

"Mom." Todd stood in the middle of the kitchen floor and spoke in a tone that made Della look up quickly and brace herself. "Mom, there's a letter—from Grandpa!"

Della looked at her son curiously. He would not make jokes about this.

"Grandpa?" whispered Liza. "Can they write letters from heaven?"

Todd studied the letter. "It's from Jerusalem."

"Liza." Della's voice was very even. "Get your father."

James sat on the couch with the unopened letter in his hands, turning it over and over. "It must have been put on a boat instead of an

airplane by mistake, and then gotten lost almost a year!"

"I heard on the news about a letter that was lost for thirty years," Todd said. "It just showed up in somebody's mailbox like nothing had happened."

"Open it, Daddy!" Liza, sitting on the floor, wriggled closer.

James continued to turn the letter over and over and then scrutinized the postmark again. "February tenth."

"Five days before he died," observed Della.

"Are you going to open it, Daddy?"

"I . . . I suppose I will."

But he sat there, holding the letter and not speaking. The other three did not speak either. Never, except during the middle of the night, had the Young household been so quiet. A teardrop fell from James's cheek and landed on the long-lost letter. He wiped his face with the back of his hand. "Sorry."

Della squeezed his arm and stood up. Still not

speaking, she lifted a candle from the mantle, lit it, and placed it on the floor in the center of the little group. Then she sat back down by her husband and put a hand on his knee.

Very carefully, as if he were performing a delicate and important operation, James opened the envelope. A second, smaller envelope with some block printing on it slipped out from the folded letter and fell to the floor. Todd picked it up and read out loud: "A Newly Discovered Text by Jesus." He handed the envelope to his father. "What's a text?"

"A writing."

James unfolded the letter.

"My dearest family." His voice broke and he paused and wiped his cheek before beginning again. "My dearest family. I have been thinking of you so much lately. We are having a wonderful time over here, poking around in ancient sites and museums and libraries, admiring one treasure after another.

"But I find myself thinking of my real

treasure—the four treasures that I love more than anything. You know that, don't you? Do you know how much I love you?"

James paused and looked at the three faces looking at him. Liza nodded, her eyes wide and filled with tears. Todd bit his lip and nodded too.

Della whispered quietly, "Oh, yes."

James cleared his throat and continued reading. "But sometimes I feel you are not happy. Sometimes I feel that, even though there is all the love in the world available, you are going without. I find myself thinking about that tonight as I sit alone in my little hotel room in Jerusalem.

"So I am sending you a gift. You will find it inside this little envelope. I have sent you things from my travels all over the world but nothing that is nearly as important as this. It is a newly discovered text by Jesus on how to have a happy marriage, how to have a happy family, and, in fact, how to have a happy world. I want you to open the envelope now and read

it, and then come back to this letter."

Looking over at his wife, James put down the letter and picked up the smaller envelope. *A newly discovered text?* he thought. Had the archaeology expedition discovered something that they didn't know about? Something amazing like the Dead Sea Scrolls or the Nag Hamadi Library? They hadn't read anything in the paper about such a find.

James opened the second envelope and took out another sheet of paper. He unfolded it and read out loud: "Therefore all things whatsoever ye would that men should do to you, do ye even so to them."

The other three waited.

"That's all?" Todd asked.

"That's all."

"But that's not new!" said Todd. "That's old. Real old! It's the Golden Rule. Do unto others as you would have others do unto you. Everybody knows that."

James picked up the letter again and continued

reading. "I think I just heard someone say, 'But that's not new—that's old!'"

Todd and Liza both looked around the room, as if searching for a ghost.

"Yes, it is old. But it is being newly discovered every day. I rediscover it frequently. When your Grandma and I discovered it together, it made all the difference in the world in our marriage and in our whole lives.

"If you think it's just words, you're wrong. It's a formula for a miracle. And I want you to do something for me. Will you do it?"

Liza and Todd both nodded as if hypnotized.

"This is what I am asking of you, my treasures. I want you to sit down together, all four of you, and look at each other in silence, and say to yourself, 'If I were that person, how would I like to be treated?' Just think about it. Open your mind and your heart, and you will know. And then, if you act on it, you will see the miracle happen.

"This is what I want for you because I love

you more than anything. And this is what Jesus wants for you because he loves you even more than I do.

"I look forward to being with you next Christmas. I will be there. Nothing can ever happen to me that can keep me from being with you at Christmas.

"Until then, love always, from Grandpa and Jesus."

Slowly, James put down the letter and again wiped his eyes with the back of his hand. For a moment—a long, unusual moment—everything was still, as still perhaps as one far star appearing in a dark sky. No one spoke. For at least twenty minutes they sat there looking at one another, the little candle between them offering a steady, golden glow.

Chapter Four

When the family got up and went about the business of the day, you couldn't tell that anything really amazing had happened. James went back to the garage. Della and Liza went back to the kitchen to bake and frost the Christmas cookies. And Todd went over to a friend's house to practice basketball.

But again, don't let appearances fool you. Look a little deeper.

Look at Todd, sitting at the supper table, actually allowing Liza's elbow to almost touch his shoulder and saying absolutely nothing about it.

Look at Liza, watching Todd spill milk in the front room where he wasn't supposed to take it anyway, and not running to tell Mom.

Look at James, looking at Della over the top of his newspaper, studying her as if he was studying a classified ad for something he was really interested in.

And look at Della, looking at James asleep on the other side of the bed, with just enough moonlight coming in the window to remind her that the older he got the more he looked like his father.

Della turned on her little reading lamp by the bed and reached over her husband for the letter that he had placed on his bedside table. She didn't have to put on her glasses to read it; in fact, she didn't even have to read it. She could almost hear a sweet, deep voice reading it to her. Grandpa? Jesus? "Therefore all things whatsoever ye would that men should do to you, do ye even so to them."

What did she wish that James would do for

her? Oh, understand her! To try to come into her life, her mind, and to know who she really was—know what she felt, what made her cry, what made her smile, and what made her love to be in her garden.

She wanted James to come and spend an hour with her in her garden, just sitting there on the bench he built by the angel she bought. She wanted him to sit there, holding her hand, and notice how the roses and poinsettias were doing and ask her how she liked that book he had seen on her bedside table. She wanted to be told that looking in her eyes was like looking in the skies or like looking into blueberry pies. He used to be silly, and she loved it.

"Whatsoever ye would that James should do to you, do ye even so to him." What? Enter into *his* mind, into his closed and unexpressive heart? Enter into—ah, no! Enter his dark and threatening cave? No! But . . .

Maybe it happened because she was half asleep and her usually guarded borders were

relaxed. It felt like a little warm spot moved around and around inside her heart and grew until it could not be contained. Then it slipped right out from the middle of her chest and danced a path across the bedsheets, slipping into the heart of her husband. And it stayed there the rest of the night, the path it had pioneered moving warmth back and forth between them. When Della woke up, she woke with a start, feeling that she had gone on a strange quest and had come back with a full heart—a heart so full it was spilling out of her hands.

She watched James shave, watched him get dressed to go to work. She watched as if she had not seen this hundreds of times. He didn't *want* to go, but he was going, and without a grumble. He was going to go out and talk about insurance all day to people that he didn't really want to talk to just so he could make the mortgage payment and buy food for his family. Gratitude crept over her like a soft blanket that a mother pulls over a sleeping child.

James hung his wet towel on the rack instead of dropping it on the floor like some men do. And he put the toilet seat down. Her cousin Marilyn was absolutely certain that her husband did not love her because he never put the toilet seat down no matter how many times she told him it was a symbolic and very important thing. But James put the toilet seat down, and that meant a lot.

Then, as she studied him tying his shoelaces, she had two thoughts. She thought that it was harder for him to bend over than it used to be because he ate more and exercised less than he really should, and she'd told him a hundred times. . . . Her second thought was, *So what? The world will little note nor long remember the few extra pounds on my husband.*

And then—and this was very strange—Della felt that she was looking past her husband's exterior into something else. It was a bit like staring at one of those posters with only squiggly lines, when suddenly you refocus and there is a

universe of stars and the sun and moon. As Della stared at her husband, she suddenly had a tiny glimpse, a glimpse that took her breath away, of the shining inhabitant of that overweight, slightly balding, middle-aged body. Something like awe stirred in her, and an impulse rose in Della that was strong—an impulse from her full heart flowing into her waiting hands, an impulse to give him something grand. *This must be what the wise men felt as they considered their gifts and gathered their gold, frankincense, and myrrh,* she thought. *What wondrous thing can I give to James?* She thought of the sweater she had seen at Ross's Discount Clothing. It was nice, but what would make his face light up with just a bit of the brilliance she had seen hidden inside him? How could she "Do unto James?" If she were him. . . .

Of course!

As Della drove into the Sears parking lot, it was packed with Christmas shoppers. She found herself humming along with the holiday music as she hustled through the women's and shoe departments to find the tool department.

She had always felt as though she were on enemy territory whenever she passed through this department. It had felt like one big garage, and she hated the garage. But here she was, saying to the young man, "Yes, you may help me. I want a table router and a set of high-speed router bits. Ball bearing. Top grade."

"He's got a table saw?" asked the young man. "Without a table saw these won't do you much good."

"Oh, he's got the table saw, all right. Which of these do you recommend?"

"No question. This baby right here."

"Hmmm. How much?"

"Three seventy-five."

Something told Della that did not mean three dollars and seventy-five cents. "Three *hundred?*"

"And seventy-five. This other one is forty dollars less, but it doesn't have . . ."

"No, no, I want the best."

"Well, this is it!" The young man patted the router and bits as a mother proudly pats her child.

Della felt the wallet in her coat pocket. In it were thirty-five dollars and a maxed-out credit card. What would the wise men have done if they'd had only a few shekels and no credit with the frankincense seller? Well, they'd have been wise enough to figure *something* out.

"I'll be back." Della turned hastily from the young man and made her way to the nearest exit.

So that nobody would ask questions, Della popped some popcorn in the kitchen and put on one of the kids' favorite videos. Then she got an old blanket and hurried out to her garden. Like a thief or a kidnapper, not giving any time for

second thoughts, Della threw the blanket over her marble angel and slowly lifted it. It easily weighed thirty pounds. Carefully, she carried it over the rocks and then set it gently onto the back seat of the car.

When Mr. Greeley saw her carrying her large bundle into his store, he ran to help her.

"Ah," he said, "Mrs. Young! You've come to select a stand for the angel?"

"No," Della replied, smiling. "I've come to sell the angel."

"Ah!" Insight, followed by confusion. "Sell? Has the angel been a bad angel?"

"She's wonderful. But there's something—something very important that I have to buy. How much could you pay for her?"

"Hmm. Well, as I have said, you don't find one like her every day. Hmm. Three hundred."

"And seventy-five?" Della whipped the blanket off the lovely piece of marble. "Look at that incredible work!" Surely wise men would drive a good bargain.

Mr. Greeley laughed. "And seventy-five!"

As Della left Greeley's Art and Monument with empty arms and a large wad of cash in her wallet, she was amazed. She had just lost her angel, and she was more excited than on the day she found her. She felt like a wise man who had sold a camel to buy frankincense for the Christ child.

The young man at Sears counted out Della's six fifties, three twenties, one ten, and five ones. "You rob a bank, lady? Am I going to see your face on the news tonight?"

Della smiled wickedly. "You wait and see."

Three-dollars and fourteen cents was all she had left of her original thirty-five dollars once sales tax was paid.

Della hurried to her car, carrying a large box in both arms and a little brown bag tucked under her chin, a bag full of three dollars and

fourteen cents worth—minus tax—of chocolate peanut clusters.

Just before James was expected to drive in from work, the job was done. The table router and bit set was gift-wrapped perfectly and hidden beneath the bench in Della's garden, covered by plastic bags in case it rained. Nobody would find it because nobody ever went there besides her.

Chapter Five

When Christmas Eve finally came, Della had hardly been able to sleep for five nights, imagining James's face when he unwrapped the present, imagining his voice when he could finally speak. She went through her days smiling, and she was sure that her secret shone in her eyes. Surely everyone must know.

She found herself doing the strangest things. When the children quarreled—and was she imagining it or were their fights fewer and quieter?—she discovered a little store of energy in what used to be an empty place inside of her, and she found herself bursting into song and ignoring their squabbles.

Every time she saw James, she had to hide

her secret smile. When she watched him go out to his cave, she didn't even mind! Being in the garage seemed to make him happy, and she *wanted* him to be happy! She curled up on the couch alone and looked at the Christmas tree lights and felt warmed. This was a new feeling. No, this was an old feeling. This is how she felt a long time ago, when she was in love! Back then James could be far away, but he was as close as the air she breathed, and it was delicious.

A time or two she surprised herself—and no doubt the inhabitant of the cave—by opening the door and calling out sweetly, "Hey, lights out, lights out! Don't you know it's *bedtime?*"

In recent years, Della had hoped the kids would sleep in on Christmas morning, but this year she was the first one awake, and she grabbed her pillow and pummeled James with it, singing, "Deck the James with boughs of

pillows, tra la la la la, la la, la la! Got to wake this sleeping fellow, tra la la la la, la la, la la! Merry Christmas!"

James grinned and drew her into his arms. "Who is this wild woman?"

"Woman who runs with reindeer! Get up! Get up!"

They had not had a pillow fight in years, and their laughing and hollering brought the children running.

"Mine first! Mine first!" Liza grabbed a present from under the tree.

"Okay, Liza," said her father. "You open one first."

"No! I mean my present to Todd first. Here!" She held out a gaudily wrapped, over Scotch-taped package to her brother. "Open it! Open it!"

Todd ripped open the paper and jumped as something brown and multilegged fell into his lap. "Yikes!" It was the largest plastic spider he had ever seen.

"Don't you like it?" asked Liza with real

concern on her face. "It was the ugliest one I could find!"

Della and James burst into laughter, and Todd joined them.

"Yeah! Sure! It's way cool! Thanks!" He took the spider and brandished it in front of Liza's face.

Liza put her hands on her hips and looked at him through narrow eyes. "You can't scare me. I already named him. His name is Marvin. Hi, Marvin."

Everyone laughed again, and Todd dived under the tree and came up with a box wrapped in red paper with a large gold ribbon. No one had ever seen a ribbon on a present from Todd before.

"Whoa!" said his father. "What's the occasion?"

"Christmas!" Todd said and handed the present to his sister.

Liza took the package and sat down on the floor. Carefully she pulled off the tape and uncovered the box, lifted the lid and let out a

soft, "Oh!" Then she picked up a doll—a little Indian doll with a baby on her back and real feathers and beads on her real buckskin dress. "Oh! She's beautiful!"

Todd beamed. "Neat, huh? That's real buckskin, you know."

"Where did you get her?"

"Traded Joey's sister for some baseball cards and a pocket knife."

Della could wait no longer. She knelt by the tree and from under some smaller packages, slid out a large, carefully wrapped box. "Hmm. What can this one be?" She lifted the tag and read, "To James, with all my love, from Della." She pushed the box to her husband. "Must be for you. Kind of heavy."

Paying little attention to the superb job of wrapping, ribboning, and curling that had taken Della half an hour at least, James tore open the paper.

"What is it, Dad?"

"Let me see, Daddy!"

James did not reply. He could not speak. He just sat there with the box in his lap, staring at it as if the words on the box were Russian instead of the plain English that said, "Table Router."

"What's it for, Dad?"

"It's . . . it's . . ." James put the box on the floor and reached over and took his wife in his arms, laughing, but with a catch in his voice he said, "Aah! Aah, Della!"

"Do you like it, James?"

"How in the world? This cost *money!*"

"Oh, I managed."

"No, *really*, Della. How?"

Della paused and then smiled shyly. "Well, I went all over town, but nobody would buy my hair, so I sold my angel. But I wanted to!" she added hastily. "Oh, James, I had such fun buying this for you. Don't tell me I shouldn't have done it. Angels are for bringing happiness and that's what mine did. Don't you like it?"

James stared at her with an odd expression

on his face. "You, you sold your angel?"

"Yes. She's gone. Flown away! Don't be angry with me, James. I had to do unto you something wonderful this Christmas. I had to!"

"Oh, Della. I'm not angry! I'm just . . ." Then he began to laugh. "Close your eyes."

Della closed her eyes and sat quietly on the couch as she heard the door to the garage open, close, and open again. She heard a thud in front of her. James said, "Ta-dum!"

Della opened her eyes to see something large and round and wrapped. It was hard. She tore off the paper and gasped. There in front of her was a sparkling, eighteen-inch, delicately carved marble stand—the perfect stand for her vanished angel!

"Oh!" Tears mixed with laughter as Della reached out and ran her fingers over the cool, white surface. "Oh, James," she whispered. "It's stunning! How? Where did you get the *money?*"

"Well. It's kind of an interesting story. In

fact, a *really* interesting story. I . . . I sold my table saw."

Della stared at him strangely, as if he were speaking Russian and not the plain English in which he had just told her that his table saw was gone—sold to get the money to buy the stand for the angel that she had sold to get the money to buy a router for his table saw.

She threw herself into his arms. "Your table saw! Oh, James! But you loved it so!"

"It's okay. I need a little time out from the shop. I thought I'd come out and spend a little time with the two angels in the garden. Only now I'll just get the one angel. But that'll be okay. She's the best."

For the first time in their fourteen years together, James had more words than Della. All she could say through her tears was, "Okay."

Todd and Liza could hardly believe what they saw next—their mother and father laughing out loud and rolling on the floor. And then kissing. Actually, really, honestly kissing!

Grandpa would have enjoyed that Christmas day. Well, he did, of course. A spirit as great and grand as Grandpa would not let a little thing like death get in his way. Jesus was there too. You know that death is nothing to him. They had both promised, and they were there.

And if you think that you were not there too, you are mistaken. The same cosmic cord that joined those four unsuspecting souls like a strand of Christmas lights goes on and on and on and connects every blessed being in the universe in a great round of One, beyond time and space. When four become brighter, it brightens all. Your magnificence and my magnificence are multiplied by the giving that went on that Christmas day in the Young household: the gifts from the splendid and sometimes still obnoxious twelve-year-old boy, and from the beautiful and occasionally still whining eight-year-old girl, and from the awesome, loving, and now and then

still insensitive husband and wife, each of whom had found a remarkable recipe for happiness in a newly discovered text by Jesus Christ.

About the Author

Carol Lynn Pearson has been a professional writer, speaker, and performer for many years.

In addition to her volumes of poetry, she is well known for such books as *Goodbye, I Love You*; *Consider the Butterfly*; and *A Stranger for Christmas.*

Carol Lynn has been a guest on such programs as *The Oprah Winfrey Show* and *Good Morning America* and has been featured in *People* magazine.

She has a master of arts degree in theater, is the mother of four grown children, and lives in Walnut Creek, California. You can visit her at www.clpearson.com.

0 26575 12081 3